VEGAN FRENCH
FAVORITES

SARALA TERPSTRA

VEGAN FRENCH FAVORITES

30 beloved French recipes reimagined

RECIPES AND PHOTOGRAPHY
BY
SARALA TERPSTRA

COVER DESIGN
BY
PHOEBE OUMA

CONTENTS

Introduction 7

Noteworthy Ingredients 13

STARTERS

Carottes Râpées 19

Carrot Soup 21

Salade 22

Leeks in Vinaigrette 23

Walnut Pâté 25

MAINS

Artichoke Sandwich 28

Beet Tartare 30

Buckwheat Galettes 32

Cassoulet 34

Cauliflower au vin 37

Crêpes 39

    Gluten-Free Rice Flour Crêpes 40

    Chocolate Spread 41

Croque Monsieur 42

Eggplant Meunière 44

Fondue Savoyarde 47

Gratin Dauphinois 48

Mushroom Bourguignon 51

Onion Soup 53

Quiche Lorraine 55

Ratatouille 57

Salade Niçoise 59

Spinach Soufflé 60

Tomates Farcies 62

Tomato Tart 64

    Socca Crust 65

Vegetable Parmentier 66

DESSERTS

Cherry Clafoutis 69

Chocolate Fondants 70

Crème Brûlée 72

Lemon Sorbet 75

Mousse au Chocolat 77

Tarte Tatin 79

INTRODUCTION

WHEN I ADOPTED A PLANT-BASED DIET out of concern for the planet and my health, I missed French cooking. Cooking has always been my love language, and cooking French cuisine is one of my favorite ways to immerse myself in French culture. As the world went into lockdown in the spring of 2020, I suddenly found myself with the time to explore vegan French cuisine. Out of excitement over the recipes I was coming up with and a desire to connect with the outside world during the lockdown, I began a blog on Instagram (follow me @saralaterpstra if you'd like to keep up with my latest recipes and life in France). Since then, I have spent every day experimenting, failing, succeeding, and learning. While I am constantly evolving as a cook and realize I will spend a lifetime studying French cuisine and not know it all, I have learned some basic principles of vegan French cooking. This little cookbook is a way to share my "tools."

I am not French but I became smitten with France long before I adopted a plant-based lifestyle. Growing up in a multicultural family in both the United States and India, I had little to no exposure to French food and culture and yet, was never fully satisfied with my own. Being raised in two worlds piqued my curiosity for other cultures from a young age. So when I visited France the summer after I graduated from high school, I was enamored. The language, style, architecture, wine, and food were not only different from what I knew but also executed so well- as if to say, "every little bit matters!". It felt like I was on the outside looking in and I longed to be a part of this special world. It has been over a decade since my first trip to France. Since then, I've had the opportunity to study in, travel in, and finally move to France! My curiosity for other cultures has also led me to explore the world in the past decade, jumping at any opportunity to visit or live in a new city or country,and chronically moving…but France has my heart.

But how can you love French culture and its food without meat and dairy? You might wonder. While it is true that French cuisine is well known and well loved for its endless variety of cheese and its rich meat dishes, I have found there is much more to French cuisine than the cholesterol-laden stereotypes. With the focus on eating seasonally in France, French cooking has an appreciative relationship with vegetables. The markets mark the changing of the seasons, as on each visit you may find different produce available. Marketgoers will chat enthusiastically with vendors about how best to cook a certain variety of mushrooms. *With butter, garlic, and parsley* is a common answer I've received. The same way you might cook a steak, fish, or snails. It is the French *way* that is enamoring and that I seek to share in this

7

book. The concepts of French cooking, when applied to plants, create dishes that are at once novel and timeless. The story of how the food was sourced, fresh and high-quality ingredients, balance, attention to presentation and detail, carving out time for meals, eating slowly, and the pride and joy taken in a good meal-this is what it means to me to eat the French way.

Vegetables are celebrated in France but the most famous French recipes tend to be heavy on meat and dairy. I wanted this book to be a resource for those who want to enjoy French classics without animal products, so the recipes are reimagined versions. But I have done my best to sanctify the traditional concepts. I am not the first to veganize French cooking. With plant-based lifestyles on the rise, there are plenty of vegan French bloggers and chefs in the French-speaking world. There are also plenty of English-speaking bloggers and chefs who make the occasional vegan French recipe. But for some reason, even though the vegan cookbook market has exploded, vegan French cookbooks in the English market are severely lacking. Considering that French cuisine is one of the most influential in the world, it certainly deserves its place in the mainstream vegan scene. So here is my contribution to a worthy cause. And as a non-French person, it comes from a place of admiration, respect, and that of a humble learner.

This little cookbook has just thirty recipes, but it offers a well-rounded introduction-a glance, at vegan French cooking. With five starters, nineteen mains, and six desserts, the recipes have been carefully selected to demonstrate a variety of plant-based cooking techniques while allowing you to enjoy some of the most famous and beloved French dishes. Most of the recipes are gluten-free, and gluten-free substitutions have been included for those that are not. As a proponent of a whole-food, plant-based diet, you will find my recipes avoid processed foods and use less oil than is traditional, and for most of the savory recipes I have left the salt measurements to your own tastes. I hope each recipe will nourish, inspire, and make you feel....

...as if you were in France

WHETHER FOR THE FIRST TIME OR EVERY DAY, cooking vegan food can be a joyful and exciting experience. I was recently asked how cooking French has changed the way I approach vegan food. The simple answer is that a French approach has created even more excitement and joy. The following are practices that I've observed and admired in France and try to implement wherever I am. I share them, not as a list of rules or to tell you that the French do everything better (they eat frozen food too), but to add warmth and fun to the recipes, if you wish.

Use Quality Ingredients

Whether in large cities or small towns, the markets in France are personal, charming, and overflowing with the most beautiful fruits and vegetables I've seen. I actually enjoy shopping at the markets in France, whereas large, neon supermarkets make me feel like getting the whole tedious job over with. Thankfully, the farmers' market scene is growing in the United States and even at the supermarkets, there are an abundance of choices. Wherever it is affordable and accessible, I try to choose organic and local. I make selective splurges, such as on good olive oil or chocolate, and stubbornly avoid preservatives. I often find that fresh ingredients are just as affordable and accessible as packaged but taste much better (lemons and herbs are a good example of this). At the very least, I try to choose thoughtfulness over convenience.

Eat Outside

It is magical how much better a meal tastes outside. Being in nature helps us relax and open our senses, allowing us to enjoy our meal fully. During one summer I spent studying in France, I can barely remember having dinner inside. Those long meals outside in the sweet evening air were the highlight of that summer and made me realize that dinner could be merry every night. I now make it a point to have an outdoor dining space wherever I am- whether it is a little bistro set on a little balcony (my current situation pictured on the previous page) or a big picnic table in a big backyard. If eating outside is truly not an option for you because of weather or space, you can make sure your indoor dining space is a beautiful and relaxing area.

11

In our fast-paced world, we often cut out things that don't feel necessary- losing the enjoyment of beauty for beauty's sake. Don't save your nice dishes and tablecloths for guests. Whether you're dining outside or inside, it only takes a couple of minutes to set the table but doing so is a gift to yourself. You deserve to have a beautiful, relaxing meal every day. I like to hunt for vintage dishes, tablecloths, napkins, and candlesticks at thrift stores-they're inexpensive but look very elegant. A simple bouquet of fresh flowers gives a welcoming and cheerful touch to the dining table, especially next to a bottle of wine. On most nights, it's just my husband, toddler, and myself at dinner, but each of us enjoys a nicely set table, and it makes us more likely to slow down and spend quality time together.

Take Your Time

Instead of rushing to place the whole meal on the table, give the meal structure. Start with a glass of wine (or a refreshing drink of your choice) and a simple bite-such as olives or crackers, in your living room, backyard, or somewhere you like to sit and relax. This time is called *apéro* and will help you unwind from your day while piquing your appetite. Then move to the table and have your starter. You can always just have a salad for your starter. Salads are traditional in everyday French meals but also ideal for a plant-based diet as they are easy to make and can be dressed up a thousand different delicious ways to add more nutrients and protein to a meal (think-beans, nuts, seeds, vegetables, fruit). Soups, warm or chilled depending on the weather, also make easy and nutritious starters. Next, the main course. Garnishing with a snippet of fresh herbs is effortless but adds some grandeur. Dessert can just be fresh fruit, a square of dark chocolate, or a decadent cake- either way, sit and enjoy it.

NOTEWORTHY INGREDIENTS

VEGANIZING FRENCH CUISINE, OF COURSE, REQUIRES SOME CREATIVITY, open-mindedness, and substitutions. I consider the following ingredients my 'Vegan French Toolbox'. The recipes in this cookbook have been carefully selected to demonstrate the wonders of these ingredients and inspire you to use them in your own creations.

AGAR POWDER is vegan gelatin made from seaweed. It is a natural food commonly used as a weight-loss supplement. Agar powder is extremely versatile, easy to use, and an important tool in the vegan kitchen. It can be used to give shape and texture to vegan cheeses, mousses, and spreads and is an essential ingredient in the Walnut Pâté, Fondue Savoyarde, Crème Brûlée, Lemon Sorbet, and Mousse au Chocolat. Agar powder may also be referred to as agar-agar and sold in the form of flakes. You can find agar at health food stores or online.

AQUAFABA is the humble liquid in a can of chickpeas or garbanzo beans. The liquid from home-cooked chickpeas can also be used. When chilled and whipped with cream of tartar, aquafaba turns into a foam resembling egg whites and is used in vegan mayonnaise, whipped cream, mousses, and baked goods. Aquafaba is only used in the Mousse au Chocolat recipe, but if you're unfamiliar with it, I recommend looking up and trying other recipes with aquafaba- you'll be amazed!

COCONUT CREAM, which solidifies when cool and melts when warm, makes a delicious replacement for heavy cream and butter in vegan recipes, giving richness without little to no coconut flavor. Coconut cream is usually found in cans or cartons in the baking or international section at grocery stores. It is also readily available at Asian grocery stores. Some brands use additives, but pure coconut cream tastes better. Organic coconut creams always seem to work well. You can also buy canned coconut milk and refrigerate it; the cream will separate from the liquid and float to the top. Skim the cream from the top and save the liquid for soups or baked goods. If you are very averse or allergic to coconut, you can try vegan butter in place of coconut cream. Coconut cream is used in the Quiche Lorraine, Cherry Clafoutis, and Crème Brûlée.

CHICKPEA FLOUR is made from dry, ground chickpeas or garbanzo beans and can be found in the baking or gluten-free section at grocery stores. I buy it at my local Indian grocery store, where it is referred to as *besan* and sold in bulk for a good value. Chickpea flour makes an excellent gluten-free egg replacer in vegan quiches, crêpes, and baked goods with its protein, mild flavor, and binding properties. Chickpea flour is used in the Buckwheat Galettes, Gluten-free Rice Crêpes, Quiche Lorraine, and Socca.

COGNAC is a French brandy that is widely available and naturally vegan. Cognac is often used in French cooking to deepen the flavors of sauces, meats, and desserts. Cognac can easily be found in the liquor section of grocery stores and is used in the Walnut Pâté and Cauliflower au Vin.

14

DIJON MUSTARD not to be replaced with American yellow mustard - is specifically French mustard, made with wine. It has a sharp, distinct flavor and is an essential ingredient in many of the recipes in this book. Although Dijon mustard is made in France, it is widely exported and found in the condiment section of grocery stores. It is important to note that some Dijon mustard brands are not vegan.

HERBES DE PROVENCE is a blend of dried herbs and spices commonly found in Provence, in the South of France. The blend is comparable to an Italian Seasoning blend but has a distinctly French flavor. While the addition of lavender in some blends is controversial, I personally love the aroma and flavor the lavender gives. Herbes de Provence can be found in the spice section at supermarkets or health food stores. Herbes de Provence is used only used in the Vegetable Parmentier in this book, but it can be added to soups, stews, and roasts and is worth having in the kitchen.

HERBS such as bay leaves, fresh parsley, and fresh thyme are commonly used in French cooking. They are widely available and can make all the difference in a dish. The herbs are often tied together in a bundle called a *bouquet garni* that is added to a dish and allowed to simmer. I find that no flavor is sacrificed by adding the herbs separately. Just pull out any herb stems in the dish before serving. Fresh herbs are used in most of the savory recipes in this cookbook and are highly recommended, but dried herbs will do in a pinch.

KALA NAMAK or Indian Black Salt is actually a pinkish-grey colored salt hailing from South Asia. It is made from Himalayan pink salt and a mixture of spices and herbs. With its natural sulfuric flavor, it is commonly used as an "egg" flavoring in vegan recipes. Kala namak can be found at South Asian or Indian grocery stores, or online; and is used in the Buckwheat Galettes, Quiche Lorraine, and Spinach Soufflé.

MAPLE SYRUP is a natural sweetener that is great for deepening flavor and caramelizing. Its liquid form makes it easy to incorporate into any dish. I especially like to use maple syrup when recreating dishes that traditionally use sausage, ham, or bacon, as cured meats tend to be slightly sweet. If maple syrup is not accessible or too expensive where you live, you can substitute another liquid sweetener such as agave syrup, or use a sprinkle of sugar. Maple syrup is used in a handful of the recipes in this book.

NUTRITIONAL YEAST is a delicious and healthy vegan seasoning made from deactivated yeast and high in B vitamins. It is commonly used as a "cheese" flavoring in vegan recipes. You can find nutritional yeast in the spice or natural food section of large supermarkets or at health-food stores. Nutritional yeast is used in several of the recipes in this cookbook.

OAT MILK is perfect for vegan French cooking because of its creamy flavor. French dishes often use heavy cream or milk, for which oat milk is a good substitute. Be sure to use unsweetened oat milk. I do not recommend substituting other plant milk unless you have a dietary issue because they tend not to be as rich, and I have not tested them with these recipes. Oat milk can be found in the dairy-free section of grocery stores. Oat milk might be the most commonly used ingredient in this cookbook.

POLENTA is a simple porridge made from cornmeal and can be found in supermarkets' baking or pasta sections. It is extremely easy to make polenta, and with its fluffy, coagulated texture and ability to absorb flavor- there is no limit to how polenta can be used in vegan cooking. I regularly use it in place of scrambled eggs or in vegan quiches. Polenta is used in the Quiche Lorraine.

RICE FLOUR can be a good gluten-free substitute for wheat flour in baking. It has a rich flavor, is not too dry or too soggy, and it takes on an appealing golden hue.

Rice flour can be found in the gluten-free section of supermarkets or at Asian grocery stores. Be sure to use white rice flour for the recipes in this cookbook. In some cases, I've found rice flour superior to wheat flour in vegan recipes, such as in the Spinach Soufflé. Rice flour is used in the Gluten-Free Rice Flour Crêpes, the Spinach Soufflé, and the gluten-free version of the Cherry Clafoutis.

SAGE POWDER is an easy way to infuse an earthy, "meaty" (for lack of a better word) flavor to vegan French cooking. I always have sage powder on hand when I am veganizing French dishes that traditionally call for bacon, deli meats, or sausage. You can find dried sage in the spice section of grocery stores. Sage powder is used in the Walnut Pâté, Cassoulet, and Croque Monsieur.

SOY SAUCE is commonly used in vegan cooking to create "umami" flavor- i.e., the fifth taste, the thing that's missing. When veganizing a dish that traditionally uses meat, soy sauce can deepen and richen the taste. Fortunately, soy sauce can be found just about anywhere, but unfortunately, many soy sauces are not gluten-free. For a gluten-free soy sauce substitute, use tamari or coconut aminos and adjust the amount, if necessary, for flavor. Soy sauce is used in many of the recipes.

SMOKED PAPRIKA quickly and easily adds a strong smoky flavor to vegan dishes. But be sure the label says 'Smoked Paprika' rather than just plain old paprika. It is an essential vegan substitute for recreating recipes that traditionally use smoked meats- such as bacon and sausage. You can find smoked paprika in the spice section of grocery stores. Smoked paprika is used in several of the recipes.

TRUFFLE OIL is made from black or white truffles infused in oil and has a rich, earthy, pungent flavor. It adds depth to vegan cheeses and is a good vegan substitute for duck or duck fat in French cooking. A little truffle oil goes a long way, so don't be put off by the seemingly high price for a small bottle. One bottle of truffle oil can easily last a year. Truffle oil can be found in the oils section of supermarkets or at specialty and import grocery stores. Truffle oil is used in the Cassoulet, Fondue Savoyarde, Mushroom Bourguignon, and Vegetable Parmentier but feel free to use it in other savory recipes as you see fit, as it's almost always complementary!

STARTERS

Carottes Râpées

Carottes râpées or grated carrot salad is so easy to make but so obviously a good idea, that you'll wonder why you never thought of it. Start with grated carrots (you can also use a spiralizer), a vinaigrette, and fresh parsley and finish there or dress it up. Garlic, shallots, olives, pickled onions, tomatoes, fresh basil, and raisins all complement this classic French salad. Balsamic vinegar is an excellent swap for lemon juice and mustard. Feel free to adjust the vinaigrette proportions as you see fit. The salad tastes especially good after marinating in its vinaigrette for a while.

4 servings

4 medium-sized carrots
2 tablespoons freshly squeezed lemon juice
2 tablespoons Dijon mustard
1 tablespoon or more olive oil
¼ cup fresh parsley, chopped
Salt to taste

1. Peel and rinse the carrots.
2. Grate the carrots into a salad bowl.
3. Mix the lemon juice, Dijon mustard, olive oil, and parsley in a small bowl to make a dressing.
4. Pour the dressing into the carrots and stir well, so the carrots are fully coated. Stir in the fresh chopped parsley.
5. Add salt to taste and then serve immediately or place in the fridge until ready to serve.

Carrot Soup

Potage Crécy or pureed carrot soup is named after Crécy, in northern France, which is said to have the best carrots in the country. However, any old-fashioned carrots will work in this recipe; it's frankly hard to mess up. Olive oil and oat milk replace the traditional butter and heavy cream for a rich silky soup. Some versions of the soup are made with rice instead of potatoes.

Pureed soups are an easy, healthy way to add a French touch to vegan cooking. This Carrot Soup models an infinite number of soups you could make by simply boiling and blending vegetables (raw vegetables are refreshing in the summer)- with a little, or a lot, of seasoning. I'll generally use whatever vegetables I have on hand, and season the soup with fresh or dried herbs, garlic, onion, vinegar, spices, and/or oat milk and sometimes include lentils, beans, or tofu. Pureed vegetable soups can be served warm or cold depending on the season, always add nutrition to a meal, and as a plus-they look elegant.

4 servings

1 tablespoon of olive oil
1 medium onion, chopped
2 cloves garlic, minced
4 carrots, chopped
1 large potato, peeled and chopped
2 ½ cups / 600 ml water
¼ cup / 60 ml oat milk
½ teaspoon apple cider vinegar
Salt and pepper to taste

1. Heat the olive oil in a medium-sized soup pot, then add the onions and fry till they are golden and lose their raw odor.
2. Add the garlic and fry for 30 seconds.
3. Add the carrots, potatoes, and water and simmer, covered, for 20 minutes.

4. Transfer to a blender and puree until smooth. Pour back into the soup pot.
5. Stir in the oat milk and vinegar and bring the soup to a boil.
6. Turn off the heat and add salt and pepper to taste.
7. *Optional step:* Drizzle a little oat milk into each bowl of soup to garnish.

Salade

If you have dined out in France, chances are you've had une salade. A simple salad is often offered as an accompaniment to your meal in French restaurants. Fundamentally, it is green or mixed green lettuce with a vinaigrette -sometimes with additions such as goat cheese, walnuts, fruit, or other vegetables. Traditionally, salad is served after the main course, but it can also be served as a starter or alongside the main course.

Consider this simple salad your go-to side for any of the main courses in this book. Enjoy it as it is, or use it as a base and add beans, nuts, seeds, vegetables, and/or fruit to complement the main course and add more protein to a meal. I use less oil than the traditional vinaigrette but feel free to use more. On the other hand, if you'd like avoid oil altogether you can swap in plant milk or mashed avocado. It's far from traditional but it tastes good.

4-6 servings

1 small head crunchy green lettuce or mixed lettuce of choice
2 tablespoons Dijon mustard

1 teaspoon red wine vinegar
1 tablespoon or more olive oil
A handful of fresh herbs, finely chopped (parsley, basil, and thyme work well)
Salt and pepper to taste

1. Chop and rinse the lettuce. Spin the lettuce in a salad spinner or pat dry.
2. In a large salad bowl, whisk together the Dijon mustard and red wine vinegar.
3. Drizzle in the olive oil a little at a time while whisking until a thick dressing is formed.
4. Add the lettuce and fresh herbs to the dressing in the bowl and sprinkle generously with salt and pepper.
5. Use a large spoon and fork to mix the dressing up into the salad until the salad is fully coated.
6. Serve the salad immediately.

Leeks in Vinaigrette

Poireaux vinaigrette or leeks in vinaigrette is a classic Parisian bistro starter. Leeks are trimmed and boiled until tender, then served at room temperature after being drizzled in a tangy vinaigrette. Small, thin leeks work best for this as they can be prepared whole and won't fall apart. While I use less oil than the traditional vinaigrette, feel free to use as much as you'd like. You can thin out the vinaigrette with water if you want to avoid oil (although I recommend using at least a little oil).

4 servings

4 large or 8 small leeks
1 shallot, minced
1 tablespoon red wine vinegar
2 tablespoons Dijon mustard
2 tablespoons or more olive oil
1 tablespoon fresh herbs, minced (thyme, parsley, and chives work well)
Salt and pepper

1. Bring a large pot of salted water to boil.
2. Cut off the top halves of the leeks, where they begin to turn green. These can be saved and used in stock. Trim just a little of the root end of the leeks, keeping the leeks intact.
3. Stand the leeks upright, position your knife in the middle of the leek and slice down ¾ of the leek. Turn the leek and make another cut across the first cut, ¾ down so that the leek has an 'x' cut and the tops fan out. Carefully rinse the leeks, removing any dirt from the leaves.
4. Place the leeks in the pot, cover, and simmer for about 10 minutes.
5. While the leeks cook, prepare the vinaigrette. Finely chop the shallots and mix with the remaining ingredients in a bowl.
6. Once the leeks are fork-tender, remove them from the pot and place on a clean towel to cool and drain.
7. Once the leeks have cooled, arrange them on a serving platter and spoon the vinaigrette over. If the leeks are large, you can slice them in half lengthwise before laying them cut-side down on the platter.
8. Allow the leeks to sit in the vinaigrette for at least 10 minutes before serving.

Walnut Pâté

Pâté de foie gras is a paste or spread traditionally made from fattened duck liver, but it can also be made with goose or chicken liver. The liver is cooked down with cognac, herbs, and spices; and sliced, spread, or mixed into cooking. The most common way of eating it is on a slice of toasted bread, but it can also be topped with fruit or pickled vegetables, served alongside a green salad, or spread on a sandwich. This vegan version uses walnuts and carrots in place of any animal products. Vegan gelatin (agar) gives the pâté the traditional sliceable and spreadable texture. Set on a board alongside fruit and a baguette (rice cakes or crackers for a gluten-free substitute) it makes a pretty party platter. The pâté tastes best when made a day in advance and will keep in the fridge for a few days.

6-8 servings

1 tablespoon of olive oil
½ onion, finely chopped
2 tablespoons Cognac or brandy
1 carrot, peeled and chopped
½ cup / 120 ml oat milk
½ teaspoon agar powder
½ cup / 40 g walnuts
2 cloves garlic, chopped
1 teaspoon hot sauce (Frank's or Tabasco work well)
A squeeze of fresh lemon juice
1 tsp soy sauce (substitute tamari or coconut aminos for gluten-free)
½ tsp dried sage
¼ tsp dried thyme
¼ tsp allspice
Salt and black pepper to taste

1. Heat the oil in a saucepan and fry the onion until soft and golden
2. Deglaze the onion with the Cognac and allow to cook for 1 minute.
3. Add the chopped carrots and oat milk. Cover and simmer until the carrots soften
4. While the carrots simmer, process the walnuts and garlic in a food processor into a crumble.
5. Add the agar powder to the carrots and simmer for 5 more minutes, stirring continuously.
6. Allow the saucepan contents to cool slightly, and then add to the ground walnuts in the processor. Add the remaining ingredients to the processor as well.
7. Process all the ingredients into a smooth paste, add salt and pepper to taste, and then transfer into a ramekin or bowl and chill for at least one hour or overnight.
8. The pâté can be removed from the mold before serving. Serve with toasted bread slices (or gluten-free rice cakes or crackers) and cornichons (pickles) or use as a spread on a sandwich.

MAINS

Artichoke Sandwich

I love a good French café sandwich. It is one of the first things I seek out, along with a jolt of that strong French coffee to fight the jet lag, after landing in France. If you've traveled in France, you know how the handsome sandwiches beckon at you from behind a gleaming glass counter. Ham, tuna, chicken, or cheese sandwiches are popular and are often much simpler than an American-style sandwich. Another key difference is the bread- the French sandwich bread is thick, chewy, and just very good. This artichoke sandwich is inspired by Pan bagnat, a French tuna sandwich and includes classic French sandwich elements. Remember to use good bakery bread! Outside of France, I usually have to lightly toast the bread to achieve a more French flavor.

2-4 servings

1-2 baguettes or crusty sandwich loaves (or gluten-free bread of choice)
1 (8 oz / 400 g) can of artichoke hearts
¼ cup / 30 g raw cashews
¼ cup / 60 ml boiling hot water
1 tablespoon Dijon mustard
1 teaspoon lemon juice
¼ teaspoon maple syrup
½ teaspoon onion powder
1 garlic clove, crushed in garlic press
1 cup lettuce, chopped
1 Roma tomato, thinly sliced
½ cup olives, sliced
A handful of fresh basil leaves
Salt and pepper to taste

1. Cover the cashews with boiling water and allow to soak for at least 30 minutes.
2. Dump the artichokes into a colander. Rinse the artichokes well.
3. Squeeze the artichokes to remove as much water as possible and place the artichokes in a mixing bowl.
4. To a processor- add the cashews with their water, the Dijon mustard, lemon juice, maple syrup, onion powder, and crushed garlic. Process into a smooth cream.
5. Mix the cashew cream into the artichokes until the artichokes are fully coated. Add salt and pepper to taste.
6. Slice the baguettes or sandwich loaves open and tear out some bread to make a hollow for the filling.
7. Spoon the artichoke mixture into the hollow.
8. Top the artichokes with lettuce, tomatoes, olives, and fresh basil leaves and sprinkle with a little salt and pepper.
9. Enjoy the sandwich immediately or within a few hours of making it.

Beet Tartare

Tartare de bœuf or Beef Tartare (also known as Steak Tartare) is made from cut or ground raw beef and sometimes raw egg yolk- mixed with a variety of seasonings such as onion, capers, parsley, mustard, and Tabasco. Beet Tartare has become a popular vegetarian and vegan adaptation of the classic, and I can always fall back on its simplistic charm if I have a last-minute dinner party. Avocado gives this version a rich, fatty texture and flavor, complementing the sweetness of the beets and the sharp seasonings.

Serve the Beet Tartare as an appetizer or as a light dinner accompanied with bread and salad.

4 servings

4 large beets
1 ripe avocado
1 shallot or quarter onion, finely chopped
2 tablespoons fresh parsley, finely chopped
1 tablespoon Dijon mustard
1 teaspoon hot sauce (Tabasco or Frank's work well)
1 tablespoon fresh lemon juice
4 cornichons, minced
2 cloves garlic, crushed in garlic pressed in garlic press
A handful of fresh parsley, minced
Salt and black pepper to taste

1. Cut off the tops and bottoms of the beets and peel. Rinse the beets, place them in a pot, and cover them with water. Simmer the beets, covered, for 45 minutes, add more water if needed.
2. Once the beets have cooled, chop them into cubes and place in a mixing bowl.
3. Cut the avocado in half, remove the seed, and scoop out the avocado using a spoon. Chop up the avocado.
4. In a processor, add a quarter of the chopped beets and all the chopped avocado. Process just into mush but not a smooth puree. The color of the avocado should not be visible.
5. Mix the processed beet and avocado with the beet cubes. Mix in the remaining ingredients.
6. Spoon a quarter of the beet tartare into a ramekin (you can also use a teacup, small coffee cup, or small bowl) and pack it down with a spoon. Place a plate on top of the ramekin and then flip over. Tap on the bottom of the ramekin and then lift the ramekin, leaving behind the molded tartare. Alternatively, spoon the tartare onto a plate and use the back end of a spoon to shape it.
7. Serve the tartare immediately or keep it in the fridge until it is ready to be served.

Buckwheat Galettes

Galettes Bretonnes or savory buckwheat crêpes originated from the northern Brittany region of France. They are commonly filled with cheese, ham, and egg and enjoyed alongside the local Breton cider. Where this vegan recipe requires a little prep work, it makes up for in crispy satisfaction! Baked tofu and mashed sweet potato replace the fried egg and are topped with smoky mushrooms in place of ham. Vegan cheese is very complementary, but you could also use 'buttery' avocado slices. Enjoy these alongside a salad for a light lunch or dinner (but I won't tell if you have them for breakfast! You won't be alone in that camp). Use a generous amount of oil in the pan when making the first crêpe.

4-6 servings

For the crêpes:
1 cup / 120 g buckwheat flour
¼ cup / 30 g chickpea flour
1 cup / 240 ml oat milk
1 cup / 240 ml water
1 tsp olive oil + more for greasing the pan
¼ tsp salt

For the toppings:
1 sweet potato, peeled and chopped
1 teaspoon kala namak
4-6 (½ inch thick) slices of firm tofu
6 white mushrooms, sliced
1 teaspoon maple syrup

1 teaspoon smoked paprika
Olive oil
Salt and pepper to taste
Optional: **vegan cheese or avocado**

1. Mix the buckwheat flour, chickpea flour, and salt in a mixing bowl and make a well.
2. Pour in the oat milk gradually while mixing. Stir in the water and oil and mix well. Set the batter aside for at least 30 minutes or up to a couple of hours.
3. Cover the sweet potatoes with water in a small pot. Boil, drain, and mash the sweet potatoes. Stir in the kala namak and set the sweet potatoes aside, covered, to keep warm.
4. Preheat the oven to 400 F / 200 C. Coat the tofu slices in olive oil, sprinkle with salt and pepper, place on a baking sheet, and bake for about 20 minutes. After 20 minutes, turn off the oven and leave the tofu in the oven to keep it warm while making the crêpes.
5. Heat about 1 teaspoon olive oil in a frying pan. Add the mushroom slices and fry until the mushroom liquid has evaporated. Stir in the maple syrup, smoked paprika, and salt and pepper to taste and fry the mushrooms a couple more minutes, until browned and sticky. Turn off the heat and cover the mushrooms to keep them warm.
6. Heat a large non-stick pan or well-seasoned cast-iron skillet. Use a generous amount of oil to grease the pan initially. Allow the oil to heat for a minute.
7. Use a large soup ladle to pour the batter in a large circle, pouring the perimeter of the crêpe first then working inwards in a clockwise motion. Use the bottom of the soup ladle to smear the crêpe in a circular motion, filling in any gaps. Based on your pan, it may work better to spread the batter by tilting the pan in a circular motion.
8. Place one slice of tofu in the middle of the crêpe. Place a scoop of the mashed sweet potato on top of the tofu and use the back of the spoon to smoothen the sweet potato into a semi-circular mound.
9. Gently fold in the four edges of the crêpe around the tofu, flattening them with a spatula so that the crêpe is square-shaped. Sprinkle the crêpe with a few of the cooked mushrooms.
10. Carefully slide the square crêpe onto a plate and serve. Repeat this process until the batter is used up.

Cassoulet

Cassoulet is a hearty stew, comparable to baked beans, and iconic of the southwest region of France. I was introduced to it in Carcassonne, a medieval fortified city in south-western France, after a weary and cold day of Christmas shopping. I ducked into the first restaurant I could find, only too happy to be warm and sitting, and was recommended the local specialty. The cassoulet came, bubbling in the clay pot that it is named for and is traditionally cooked in.

   While the ingredients vary by city, it is essentially white beans and a variety of meats. This vegan version uses chunky, caramelized mushrooms in place of meat but has no lack of protein, flavor, and comfort. Without the animal fat, this vegan version is better unbaked but if you wish to finish it off the traditional way by sticking it in the oven, drizzle it with some oil first.

4 servings

For the beans:
2 cups / 320 g dry white beans, soaked overnight or in hot water for an hour
2 celery branches, chopped
1 large or 2 small carrots, chopped
½ a large onion, chopped
2 cups / 480 ml vegetable broth
2 cups / 480 ml water
1 tablespoon tomato paste
1 tablespoon Dijon mustard
2 tablespoons fresh parsley, chopped
A few sprigs of fresh thyme
A dash of clove powder
Salt to taste

For the mushrooms:
8 oz / 230 g white mushrooms
1 tablespoon olive oil
½ a large onion, chopped
4 cloves garlic, minced
1 tsp smoked paprika
1 tsp dried sage
½ teaspoon truffle oil
Salt and black pepper to taste

1. Place all the bean ingredients in a large soup pot. Simmer on low heat for about an hour, covered until the beans soften.
2. While the beans are cooking, prepare the mushrooms. Gently pull the stems from the mushrooms and roughly break apart the mushrooms by hand in 2-3 "meaty" pieces. Rinse the mushrooms or wipe clean.
3. Heat the olive oil in a frying pan or skillet, then add the onions and fry until golden. Add the garlic and mushrooms and fry for another 15 to 20 minutes until the mushrooms start to brown and the liquid evaporates.
4. Sprinkle the mushrooms with the smoked paprika, sage, truffle oil, salt, and pepper, and fry for a few more minutes until the mushrooms are caramelizing.
5. Spoon the beans into one large dish or four individual dishes. Top with the mushrooms and serve immediately.

Cauliflower au vin

Coq au vin or 'Rooster in Wine' consists of chicken or rooster slow cooked in a wine sauce, often with bacon, herbs, and mushrooms. You can imagine why I elicit an, "Mmmm, what's for dinner?" from my husband whenever I make this vegan version. A flambé is part of the conventional cooking process where alcohol (usually cognac) is splashed in and set afire before burning it off- a process said to deepen the flavors. Cauliflower is used in this recipe in place of meat for chewy, browned bites that contrast perfectly with a rich stew. If you choose to flambé, be sure to do it safely. Enjoy the Cauliflower au Vin with potatoes or rice (mashed potatoes are my preference).

6 servings

For the stew:
1 tablespoon of olive oil
1 onion, sliced
3 cloves garlic minced
2 medium carrots, sliced
2 tablespoons flour (can substitute gluten-free flour)
1 cup / 240 ml dry red wine
2 cups / 480 ml vegetable broth
1 cup / 240 ml water
1 teaspoon tomato paste
1 tablespoon soy sauce (substitute tamari or coconut aminos for gluten-free)
1 bay leaf
A few sprigs of fresh thyme
2 tablespoons fresh parsley, chopped

For the cauliflower:
1 tablespoon of olive oil
1 whole cauliflower head
10 mushrooms, halved or quartered
1 teaspoon poultry seasoning (thyme, sage, marjoram, rosemary, black pepper, and nutmeg)
1 tsp smoked paprika
1 teaspoon nutritional yeast
½ teaspoon maple syrup
Salt and black pepper to taste
Optional *flambé*: 2 tablespoons cognac, brandy, or other liquor

1. Heat 1 tablespoon of olive oil in a pot, then add the onions and fry till the onions are golden. Stir in the garlic and fry for 30 seconds.

2. Mix in the carrots, then add the flour and mix well, so the vegetables are evenly coated. Fry for a minute. Deglaze by slowly pouring in the wine, using it to loosen the mixture from the pan. Allow the wine to cook for a minute.

3. Add the broth, water, tomato paste, soy sauce, bay leaf, thyme, and parsley. Cover and bring to a boil. Reduce heat to medium-low and allow the stew to simmer for 30 to 45 minutes, stirring occasionally.

4. While the stew is simmering, prepare the cauliflower. Flip the cauliflower over and, in a circular motion, cut out the core. This will allow the florets to fall off. Discard the core and cut any excessively large florets in halves or quarters, keeping most of the florets whole. Cut the mushrooms in halves or quarters.

5. Heat 1 tablespoon of olive oil in a frying pan or cast-iron skillet. Lay each cauliflower floret and mushroom in the pan and sprinkle with the poultry seasoning, smoked paprika, and nutritional yeast. Stir and then fry for a couple of minutes, allowing the cauliflower and mushroom to blacken.

6. Splash the cauliflowers and mushrooms with a little water and cook for about 5 minutes until the vegetables start to soften.

7. *Optional step*: Once the water has cooked off, pour two tablespoons of cognac or brandy all over the cauliflower and mushrooms and immediately light with a match or lighter. Allow the flames to dissipate.

8. Pour the stew into the cauliflower and mushrooms, mix gently, and stir in the maple syrup and salt and pepper to taste. Allow to simmer for a few minutes.

9. Serve the Cauliflower au Vin immediately over mashed potatoes or rice.

Crêpes

Crêpes are made from wheat flour, eggs, milk, and butter. The use of cornstarch in vegan crêpes helps to recreate the soft, chewy texture of the traditional ones. I use whole wheat flour in this recipe which creates a darker, browner crêpe, but for a more classic-looking light-colored crêpe, use all-purpose flour. The gluten-free rice flour crêpes should be made smaller than the traditional ones, using a non-stick pan. I've also included the recipe for my easy chocolate spread. It makes a healthy, vegan alternative to Nutella if you have a special place in your heart for the classic hazelnut spread

4-6 crêpes

1 cup/ 140 g wheat flour
1 tablespoon cornstarch
¼ teaspoon salt
1 cup/ 240 ml oat milk
½ cup/ 120 ml water
1 teaspoon olive oil

1. Mix the flour, cornstarch, and salt in a large mixing bowl.
2. Make a well in the flour, pour in a little oat milk, and mix with a little flour to make a paste. Continue adding a little oat milk at a time, mixing with a little flour until a thick batter is formed.
3. Slowly whisk in the water and then the oil.
4. Refrigerate the batter for one hour.
5. Heat a cast-iron skillet or non-stick pan and add some oil. Use a generous amount of oil for the first crêpe.
6. Use a soup ladle to pour some batter in a large circle, pouring the perimeter of the crêpe first then working inwards in a clockwise motion. Use the bottom of the soup ladle to smear the crêpe in a circular motion, filling in any gaps. Depending on your pan, it may be easier to spread the batter by tilting the pan in a circular motion.
7. Cook for one minute on each side (the first crêpe may take a little longer). Use a spatula to flip. Carefully slide the spatula under and around the edge of the crêpe until it loosens, then flip and cook for another minute.
8. Place the cooked crêpes on a plate and cover with another plate, or wrap them in a clean towel, to keep them from drying out until serving them.
9. Spread with the desired topping and serve.

Gluten-Free Rice Flour Crêpes

1 cup / 140 g rice flour
¼ cup / 25 g chickpea flour
1 ¼ cups / 300 ml water
¼ cup / 60 ml oat milk
¼ teaspoon salt

1. Dump the rice flour into a mixing bowl and sift in the chickpea flour. Mix in the salt.
2. Make a well in the flour and add the water gradually to form a smooth batter. Whisk in the oat milk.
3. Heat a small non-stick pan (a cast iron doesn't work well for these. Make these smaller than regular crepes to keep them from breaking).
4. Use a soup ladle to pour in some batter and tilt the pan in a circular motion, so the batter fully covers the pan.
5. Cook the crêpe for a minute or two on each side. Carefully slide a rubber spatula under and around the edge of the crêpe and flip gently.

Chocolate Spread

5 large Medjool dates, pitted
2 tablespoons raw cashews
Boiling water
1 tablespoon oat milk
3 tablespoons cocoa powder
½ teaspoon vanilla extract
A dash of salt

1. Break the dates apart, pull out the pits and place the dates and cashews in a small bowl.
2. Pour enough boiling water over the dates and cashews to just cover them and allow to soak for 30 minutes.
3. Add the dates and cashews with their water and remaining ingredients to a processor and process until smooth.

Croque Monsieur

A Croque monsieur is a toasted ham and cheese sandwich made with Gruyère cheese and béchamel- a white milk sauce. These hearty sandwiches make for an easy lunch or dinner, alongside a salad, and are a French café staple. This vegan version uses smoky, sticky sweet potatoes in place of ham and a garlic-y walnut and tofu spread in place of the cheese and sauce for a comforting sandwich the whole family will love. Topping the sandwich with vegan cheese is optional but very complementary. Vegan gouda is my preferred topping.

2 servings

4 bread slices

For the sweet potatoes:
2 sweet potatoes
1 teaspoon soy sauce
1 teaspoon olive oil

1 teaspoon maple syrup (or other sweetener)
½ teaspoon smoked paprika
¼ teaspoon sage powder
¼ teaspoon garlic powder
¼ teaspoon onion powder
¼ teaspoon black pepper
¼ teaspoon salt

For the "walnut" cheese:
¼ cup / 25 g walnuts
½ cup / 75 g firm tofu, chopped
1 teaspoon nutritional yeast
1 teaspoon lemon juice
1 clove garlic, crushed
¼ tsp salt

Optional: vegan cheese for topping

1. Preheat the oven to 400 F / 200 C.
2. Peel the sweet potatoes. Cut the sweet potatoes in half, lengthwise, then in half again so that each potato yields about 8 slices.
3. Lay the sweet potatoes in a baking dish. Drizzle with the olive oil, soy sauce, and maple syrup, and then rub into the sweet potatoes. Sprinkle with the remaining seasonings and rub them into the sweet potatoes.
4. Bake the sweet potatoes, covered, for 20- 30 minutes, until they are just soft. Leave the oven on.
5. While the sweet potatoes bake, prepare the walnut "cheese." Grind the walnuts until fine in a processor.
6. Add the remaining walnut "cheese" ingredients to the processor and grind until the "cheese" comes together into a ball.
7. Spread half of the walnut "cheese" on two slices of bread and arrange half of the sweet potatoes on the bread. Spread the sweet potatoes with the other half of the walnut "cheese," top with the other half of the sweet potatoes, then lay the other slices of bread on top to make two sandwiches.
8. If using, cover the top slices with vegan cheese.
9. Bake the sandwiches at 400 F / 200 C for 10 minutes or until they start to brown. Serve immediately.

Eggplant Meunière

Sole meunière is an uncomplicated dish of sole fish fried in butter. It was Julia Child's first meal in France-the one that made her fall in love with French cuisine. Meunière refers to the "miller's wife style," that is, dusted with flour. The fried sole is drizzled with a butter sauce, fresh lemon juice, and fresh parsley and often served with a side of boiled potatoes. It's a timeless concept that can easily be applied to vegetables, and eggplant is especially good. Thick slabs of eggplant are battered and baked until juicy,

golden, and slightly crispy and then drizzled with olive oil, fresh lemon juice, and parsley. Simple boiled potatoes on the side are perfect for mopping up the juice. A side salad with beans and/or nuts is also complimentary and adds more protein to the meal.

2-4 servings

1 large eggplant
¼ cup / 30 g all-purpose flour (or equal amount gluten-free flour)
½ teaspoon onion powder
½ teaspoon garlic powder
¼ cup water
Salt for sprinkling
1 teaspoon olive oil + more for drizzling
Fresh lemon juice
A handful of fresh parsley

1. Trim the ends of the eggplant and peel.
2. Stand the eggplant upright and slice into 4 evenly thick pieces, lengthwise.
3. Sprinkle the eggplant slices with salt on both sides and allow them to sit on a plate.
4. Preheat the oven to 400 F / 200 C.
5. In a mixing bowl, stir together the flour, water, onion powder, garlic powder, and 1 teaspoon of olive oil to make a batter.
6. Grease a large baking dish with olive oil.
7. Use your hands to fully coat the eggplant slices with the batter.
8. Lay the battered eggplant in the baking dish and bake for 20-25 minutes, until golden and crispy.
9. Lay each eggplant slice on a plate and drizzle with olive oil and fresh lemon juice. Sprinkle with fresh parsley.
10. Enjoy the Eggplant Meunière immediately with a side of boiled potatoes.

Fondue Savoyarde

Fondue savoyarde is a melted cheese dish cooked with white wine and garlic that hails from the Savoie region of the French Alps. Traditionally, the wine used in the fondue should be Savoie white wine, but if you can't find any, a good quality dry white wine will work. Kirsch (cherry liquor) is also commonly added, but I use cognac in this recipe as kirsch is harder to come by. The cashews in this vegan version create a creamy, rich flavor, while the tapioca starch and agar powder give a "cheesy" texture. The final result is a sharp, thick sauce that will glob just right on your bread. Use good bakery bread to make the toasted bread cubes for dipping and enjoy as a party dish or as part of a meal. For a gluten-free option, simple boiled potatoes to dip in place of the bread are delicious!

Serves 4-6

½ cup / 55 g raw cashews
½ cup / 120 ml boiling hot water
3 cups / 240 g chopped cauliflower
½ cup / 120 ml water
2 cups / 480 ml oat milk
1 tablespoon lemon juice
2 tablespoons nutritional yeast
1 teaspoon salt
1 clove garlic, minced
¼ cup / 30 g tapioca starch
½ tsp agar powder
¼ tsp onion powder
¼ teaspoon nutmeg powder
½ cup / 120 ml dry white wine
Optional: 1 teaspoon truffle oil
              1 teaspoon brandy

1. Pour the hot water over the cashews and set them aside to soak.
2. Place the chopped cauliflower in a pot. Add a ½ cup of water, cover, and simmer for 10 minutes or until soft.

3. In a blender- add the cashews and cauliflower with their water, the oat milk, lemon juice, nutritional yeast, salt, garlic, tapioca starch, agar powder, onion powder, and nutmeg. Blend until silky smooth.
4. In a pot, bring the wine to a boil. Pour in the blender mixture and cook for 20- 30 minutes, whisking regularly, until the fondue is thick and "cheesy."
5. If using the truffle oil and brandy, mix them in immediately after turning off the flame.
6. Transfer the fondue to a heated fondue pot or a regular serving bowl.
7. Serve with cubed, toasted bread cubes (or boiled potatoes for gluten-free) and skewers or forks for dipping.

Gratin Dauphinois

Gratin dauphinois is traditionally a dish of sliced potatoes baked in milk and cream. It is simpler than the ultra-cheesy scalloped potatoes I remember, growing up in the Midwest. But there are variations of the dish in France with the use of nutmeg, garlic, shallots, and/or cheese. This easy vegan version has a rich cauliflower cream and a sprinkle of nutritional yeast on top for a golden finish. The gratin will still be delicious without the

nutritional yeast but will bake into a greyish color rather than golden. Do not over boil the potatoes before baking, or they will turn into mush. A crunchy, fresh green salad is the perfect accompaniment.

6 servings

4-6 medium-sized potatoes, peeled
2 cups / 480 ml oat milk
¼ teaspoon nutmeg
4 cups / 350 g cauliflower, chopped
1 cup / 240 ml oat milk
2 cloves garlic
1 teaspoon lemon juice
Salt and pepper to taste
nutritional yeast for sprinkling
Olive oil for greasing the pan

1. Evenly slice the potatoes and place them in a pot. Cover with 2 cups of oat milk and sprinkle with nutmeg, salt, and pepper. Bring to a boil and simmer, covered, for 10 minutes.
2. Simmer the chopped cauliflower with 1 cup of oat milk, covered, for 10 minutes or until the cauliflower softens.
3. Transfer the cauliflower and oat milk to a processor, add the garlic and lemon juice, and puree into a smooth cream. Add salt to taste.
4. Preheat the oven to 350 F / 175 C. Lightly oil a casserole or baking dish.
5. Use a slotted spoon to spoon half the potatoes into the baking dish, leaving behind the liquid. Smother the potatoes with half the cauliflower cream.
6. Spoon the other half of the potatoes on top. Layer the potatoes at an angle, slightly on top of each other, to keep the gratin from looking too flat. Smother with the remaining cauliflower cream. Pour and spread the reserved potato liquid on top.
7. Sprinkle with nutritional yeast and bake for about 30 minutes, uncovered, until the gratin is bubbling. Serve immediately.

Mushroom Bourguignon

Bœuf bourguignon is a beef stew from the famous Burgundy wine region of France. The beef is marinated in red Burgundy wine and then slow cooked and served with a side of potatoes. Mushrooms have become a popular vegan substitute for beef in what might be the most famous French dish. The addition of lentils in this recipe adds protein and makes the stew thicker and heartier. Truffle oil richens the flavor of the mushrooms, and the crunchy fried pearl onions are the crowning glory. While pearl onions are not always easy to find, I highly recommend using them if you can. The good news is that when you're craving something rich and warming on a cold winter night, this vegan version is much faster than the traditional recipe- and you'll go to bed with a full and happy stomach.

4 servings

For the stew:
1 tablespoon olive oil
½ large onion, finely chopped
4 cloves garlic, minced
2 carrots, sliced
2 tablespoons flour (can substitute gluten-free flour)
1 cup / 240 ml dry red wine
2 cups / 480 ml vegetable broth or water
¼ cup / 50 g dry brown, green, or French lentils
2 tablespoons tomato paste
1 bay leaf
A few sprigs of fresh thyme
2 tablespoons fresh parsley, chopped
A dash of clove powder
Salt and black pepper to taste

For the mushrooms:
1 tablespoon olive oil
8 oz / 230 g mushrooms, sliced in halves
¼ tsp truffle oil
¼ tsp garlic powder
¼ tsp onion powder
1 teaspoon soy sauce

Salt
Black pepper

Topping: 1 cup/ 100 g pearl onions, peeled (to easily peel- boil the pearl onions 30 seconds then blanch in cold water. Trim the tops and squeeze the bottoms to pop out the onions from their peels)

1. Heat 1 tablespoon of olive oil in a pot. Add the onions and fry until soft and golden. Add the garlic and fry for 30 seconds.
2. Mix in the carrots, then mix in the flour and cook for a minute.
3. Pour in the wine, deglazing the pan, and using a wooden spoon to scrape up the bottom. Allow the wine to cook for a minute.
4. Add the remaining stew ingredients and simmer, covered, for 40 minutes, stirring occasionally.
5. While the stew simmers, heat 1 tablespoon of olive oil in a frying pan or skillet. Add the pearl onions and allow them to fry for about 10 minutes, till soft and browned. Set aside the pearl onions.
6. Add the mushrooms to the skillet and allow them to brown and fry until they give off their liquid. Once the mushroom liquid has evaporated, sprinkle with the garlic powder, onion powder, and truffle oil and give a good stir.
7. Splash the mushrooms with the soy sauce and allow to cook for a minute.
8. Remove the bay leaf and thyme branches from the stew and pour the stew into the mushrooms. Stir well and cook for a few minutes, adding salt and pepper to taste.
9. Spoon the Mushroom Bourguignon over potatoes or rice and top with the fried pearl onions. Serve immediately.

Onion Soup

Soup a l'oignon is a simple but delectable soup of onions simmered with stock and wine then broiled with baked bread and cheese. The onions are fried until they begin to caramelize, lending the soup a lush, sweet flavor, complemented by thyme and clove. This recipe does not stray far from the *original but uses hummus rather than cheese. Hummus and toasted bread are guaranteed to satisfy on any occasion, even more so when they're floated in onion soup (top with crackers and hummus for a gluten-free version). I use garlic hummus which contrasts nicely with the lightness of the soup.*

4 servings

2 tablespoons of olive oil
4 small or 2 large onions
1 tablespoon flour (substitute gluten-free flour)
¼ cup / 60 ml dry white wine
2 cups / 480 ml vegetable broth
1 cup / 240 ml water
A few sprigs of fresh thyme
1 bay leaf
Dash of clove powder
Salt and pepper to taste

To garnish:
½ a baguette sliced and toasted (or gluten-free crackers)
Garlic hummus (or vegan cheese for broiling)

1. Slice the onions. Heat the olive oil in a large pot and add the onions. Fry the onions for about 10 minutes, occasionally stirring, until they are soft and golden.
2. Stir in the flour and allow to cook for 1 minute. Deglaze with the wine using a wooden spoon to scrape up the bits stuck to the pan.
3. Pour in the broth and water. Add the thyme, bay leaf, and clove powder. Cover and simmer for 20-30 minutes, and then add salt and pepper to taste.
4. While the soup simmers, slice the baguette and bake the slices in the oven at 400 F / 200 C for about 10 minutes. The slices should be hard and golden.
5. Dish the soup into serving bowls. Spread hummus on the toasted baguette slices (or gluten-free crackers) and float 2-4 slices in each bowl of soup *OR* top the baguette slices with vegan cheese and broil the soup bowls in the oven until the cheese is melted. Serve immediately.

Quiche Lorraine

Quiche Lorraine is made from eggs, cream, and lardons (comparable to French bacon)-cooked in short crust pastry. It is named for the northern Lorraine region of France and can be served as a starter or main. In this recipe, polenta and chickpea flour are used for a fluffy, creamy vegan quiche. Kala namak or 'Indian black salt' gives an "eggy" flavor.

The lardons are replaced with juicy, smoky, and sweet mushrooms. The crust, made with olive oil, is a perfect balance between flaky and crispy (don't skimp on the oil in the crust!). Like the traditional recipe, the quiche is best served just slightly warm or at room temperature.

6 servings

For the crust:
1 1/4 cups / 160 g all-purpose flour (or equal amount gluten-free all-purpose flour)
½ teaspoon salt
3 tablespoons olive oil
1/3 cup / 70 ml water

For the "egg" filling:
½ cup / 85 g dry uncooked polenta
1 ½ cups / 360 ml water
½ cup / 95 g coconut cream
½ cup / 50 g chickpea flour
1 teaspoon kala namak
1 teaspoon garlic powder
1 tablespoon nutritional yeast
¼ teaspoon nutmeg
½ cup / 120 ml oat milk
1 tsp apple cider vinegar or white wine vinegar
Salt and freshly ground black pepper to taste

For the Mushroom "lardons":
1 tablespoon olive oil
8 oz / 230 g white mushrooms, chopped into cubes
1 tablespoon olive oil
1 teaspoon smoked paprika
1 teaspoon maple syrup
½ teaspoon soy sauce
Salt and black pepper to taste

1. Mix the flour and salt together in a large mixing bowl.
2. Drizzle in the olive oil, a little at a time, while mixing into the flour with your hands.
3. Add the water a little at a time, mixing with your hands, to form a slightly sticky ball of dough.
4. Refrigerate the dough for 30 minutes, then shape it in a disc and roll it out to be slightly larger than your quiche pan (you can also use a pie or tart pan).
5. Lightly grease the pan, place the dough in the pan, and use your fingers to press and shape a crust in the pan. Prick the crust all over with a fork and place it in the fridge.
6. Preheat the oven to 350 F / 175 C.
7. Bring the water and coconut milk to boil, then slowly add the polenta. Cook two minutes, stirring frequently, then set the polenta aside.
8. In a mixing bowl, mix the chickpea flour, garlic powder, nutmeg, nutritional yeast, and kala namak.
9. Stir in the oat milk and vinegar to make a thick paste. Pour the cooked polenta in and mix thoroughly.
10. Heat the olive oil in a frying pan and add the mushrooms. Allow the mushrooms to fry until they give off their liquid.
11. Stir in the smoked paprika, maple syrup, and soy sauce, and allow the mushrooms to fry for a couple more minutes until they are browned and sticky. Add salt and pepper to taste.
12. Fold the mushrooms into the polenta filling.
13. Pour the polenta filling into the prepared crust, spread, and bake for 40 minutes.
14. Allow the quiche to cool and serve just slightly warm or at room temperature.

Ratatouille

While the name may conjure up the elegant-looking dish of layered vegetables made famous by the Pixar film, Ratatouille is traditionally a rough stew of chopped vegetables. This healthy classic originates from Nice, in the South of France, and can be made with a variety of fresh vegetables- the most common being eggplant, peppers, tomatoes, and zucchini. Ratatouille is flavored with herbs, olive oil, and garlic and is one of the few recipes in this book that needs no tweaking to be made vegan. It's a timeless recipe that always feels just right- especially when made with fresh, good

57

quality vegetables. Serve the Ratatouille as a main with rice, potatoes, and/or bread, or serve chilled as a spread or dip.

4 servings

1 tablespoon olive oil
1 onion
1 red bell pepper
1 yellow bell pepper
3 cloves garlic
2 zucchinis
1 small eggplant
2 Roma tomatoes
2 tablespoons tomato paste
1 teaspoon fresh or dried thyme
A handful of fresh parsley, minced
A handful of fresh basil leaves
Salt and pepper to taste

1. Finely chop the onion and mince the garlic. Chop up the remaining vegetables in small, equal-sized pieces.
2. Heat the olive oil in a large skillet.
3. Add the onion and fry for a couple of minutes.
4. Mix in the peppers and fry for a couple of minutes.
5. Mix in the garlic and fry for 30 seconds.
6. Mix in the zucchini, eggplant, and tomato consecutively- frying each for a couple of minutes.
7. Mix in the tomato paste, fresh herbs, salt, and pepper.
8. Cover the skillet, reduce the flame to low, and allow to simmer for 30 minutes. Stir occasionally and add a splash of water if the vegetables start to stick to the pan.
9. Remove from the flame, garnish with fresh basil, and serve.
10. *Optional step:* Drizzle the *Ratatouille* with olive oil just before serving.

Salade Niçoise

Salade Niçoise is a large and colorful salad that can stand its own as a main course. The salad is named for the city of Nice, where it originated and was traditionally composed of raw vegetables, anchovies, olives, and vinaigrette. Nowadays, there are many variations of the salad, including the addition of tuna, boiled eggs, and artichokes. Boiled potatoes and green beans are widely popular as well. This recipe is standard but with chickpeas used in place of eggs for a vibrant and filling vegan take.

6 servings

1 small head Butter or Boston lettuce
1 can chickpeas, drained
1 (14 oz / 400 g) can artichoke hearts, sliced in quarters
4-6 tomatoes, sliced in quarters
2 spring onions, sliced

1 bell pepper, thinly sliced
6 radishes, sliced in rounds
A handful of black olives, whole
A handful of fresh basil leaves
Red wine vinegar
Olive oil
Salt and black pepper
Optional: boiled green beans and mini potatoes

1. Remove most of the lettuce leaves, rinse, and spin or pat dry.
2. Plate the salads individually or on a large serving platter. First, arrange the lettuce leaves as a bed on each plate or on the serving platter.
3. Layer on the remaining ingredients except for the vinegar, oil, salt, and pepper.
4. Sprinkle the salad with salt and freshly ground black pepper, then drizzle generously with vinegar and olive oil.
5. Serve the salad immediately or allow it to sit in the fridge for up to an hour.

Spinach Soufflé

A Soufflé aux épinards is a fluffy dish of egg whites baked with a flavored sauce and spinach. Soufflés can be made sweet or savory with chocolate, fruit, cheese, and vegetables. The charm of a traditional soufflé is that it must be served within minutes of coming out of the oven, after which its towering form will deflate. However, with this vegan version, there is no deflating to worry about. Made with rice flour and tofu, this vegan soufflé comes out of the oven golden and fluffy. Kala namak gives a slight "egg" flavor which complements the healthy amount of spinach. Allow the soufflé to cool slightly before serving.

4 servings

2 cups / 250 g firm tofu, chopped
Slightly less than 1 cup / 200 ml oat milk
1 cup / 120 g rice flour + more for dusting the ramekins
1 tablespoon baking powder
1 tablespoon nutritional yeast
1 teaspoon kala namak
½ teaspoon nutmeg
¼ cup / 60 ml water
1 teaspoon olive oil
8 cups / 160 g fresh spinach

1. In a processor, blend the chopped tofu and oat milk until smooth. Set aside.
2. Mix the rice flour, baking powder, nutritional yeast, kala namak, and nutmeg in a mixing bowl.
3. Stir the blended tofu into the flour mixture.
4. Stir the water and olive oil into the tofu and flour mixture.
5. Preheat the oven to 400 F / 200 C.
6. In a skillet or frying pan, sauté the spinach with a splash of water until the spinach has fully softened and the liquid has evaporated.
7. Fold the cooked spinach into the tofu and flour mixture.
8. Lightly grease 4 ramekins with oil and dump rice flour in each ramekin. Rotate each ramekin so that the inside is fully coated then dump out the excess flour.
9. Spoon the tofu and rice flour mixture into each ramekin and bake for 25-30 minutes.
10. Allow the soufflés to cool slightly before serving.

Tomates Farcies

Tomates Farcies or stuffed tomatoes make for a beautiful summer dinner or even a comforting winter dish.
The tomatoes are traditionally stuffed with ground beef, parsley, and sometimes rice and baked until juicy. The tops of the tomatoes with their stems attached are used as a garnish. This vegan version uses seasoned ground mushrooms and ground carrots in place of beef, with quinoa for protein and no lack of juicy flavor.

"They're so pretty!" my mom remarked when I brought them to a family dinner. It's the same thing I think every time I pull them out of the oven. Even though Tomates Farcies doesn't require much skill or effort, you'll feel proud when you serve them.

4 servings

1 tablespoon olive oil
1 onion
3 cloves garlic
8 oz / 230 g mushrooms, roughly chopped
1 carrot, roughly chopped
4 large or 8 small vine tomatoes
⅓ cup / 50 g uncooked quinoa
⅔ cup/ 160 ml water
1 tablespoon Dijon mustard
2 tablespoons fresh parsley, minced
1 teaspoon fresh thyme leaves
1 teaspoon soy sauce (substitute tamari or coconut aminos for gluten-free)
Salt and pepper to taste

1. Prepare the vegetables: finely chop the onion and mince the garlic. In a processor, in batches, mince the carrots and mushrooms. Set the vegetables aside.
2. Slice the tops off the tomatoes. Scoop the insides of the tomatoes into a bowl and chop up any large chunks. Set the hollowed tomatoes aside.
3. Heat the olive oil in a pot. Add the onions and fry until soft and golden.
4. Add the garlic and fry for 30 seconds.
5. Add the minced mushrooms and carrots and the insides of the tomatoes with their juice. Stir well and allow to cook for a couple of minutes.
6. Mix in the quinoa, water, and Dijon mustard. Cover and simmer for 20 minutes.
7. While the quinoa mixture is simmering, coat the hollowed tomatoes with olive oil and place them in a baking dish. Preheat the oven to 375 F / 190 C.
8. Turn off the flame for the pot and stir in the parsley, thyme, soy sauce, and salt and pepper to taste.
9. Spoon the quinoa mixture into the tomatoes, stuffing the tomatoes tightly and piling the mixture high. Place the tomato tops next to the tomatoes in the baking dish.
10. Bake the tomatoes uncovered for 20 minutes.
11. Place the tops on the stuffed tomatoes and serve.

Tomato Tart

Tarte tomate à la moutarde is a simple tart of puff pastry crust topped with mustard, tomatoes, cheese, and fresh herbs. Once the crust is sorted, a Tomato Tart makes an easy and scrumptious vegan dinner (or snack). You can use a vegan-friendly store-bought puff pastry or make the homemade vegan puff pastry crust from the Tarte Tatin recipe, which will take longer. If you choose to make the vegan puff pastry with gluten-free all-purpose flour, it will be crumbly while rolling. That's ok. Just stick any stray pieces back on the dough. Otherwise, for a healthy, gluten-free, vegan crust with less oil- why not try Socca (recipe below)? Socca is a French flatbread made from chickpeas and is naturally vegan. Traditionally it is eaten on its own as a snack, but non-traditionally it makes a delicious crust! Whatever crust you go with, the Tomato Tart tastes best slightly cooled or at room temperature.

4 servings

1 vegan puff pastry crust (store-bought OR homemade from the Tarte Tatin recipe
     OR substitute gluten-free Socca crust recipe below)
4 large vine ripe tomatoes, sliced
2 tablespoons Dijon mustard
A handful of fresh herbs, minced (parsley, basil, thyme)
Salt and black pepper

1 teaspoon- 1 tablespoon nutritional yeast
Optional: drizzle of olive oil

1. Preheat the oven to 400 F / 200 C.
2. Roll the prepared crust into a large circle. Fold-down and cinch the edges. Prick the crust all over with a fork and place it on a baking sheet or baking stone. Bake for 10 minutes.
3. Remove the crust from the oven and spread with the Dijon mustard.
4. Layer the tomatoes on the crust so that they fully cover the crust but fit neatly inside the folded edge.
5. Generously sprinkle the tomatoes with fresh herbs, salt and pepper, and nutritional yeast.
6. Optional step: drizzle the tart with olive oil.
7. Bake the tart for 20-30 minutes, until the crust is golden and the tomatoes have cooked.
8. Allow the tart to cool to slightly warm or room temperature before serving.

Socca Crust

Socca is a flatbread from Nice, in the south of France. It is made with chickpea flour, baked at high heat, and then enjoyed in slices as a snack. While it is not traditionally a crust, it makes the perfect healthy, gluten-free crust for vegan recipes. It is important to allow the socca batter to rest before baking.

1 cup / 100 g chickpea flour
1 teaspoon baking powder
¼ teaspoon salt
1 cup / 240 ml warm water
1 tablespoon olive oil

1. In a large mixing bowl, sift in the chickpea flour. Mix in the baking powder and salt.
2. Make a well in the flour and add the water gradually, mixing with the flour to avoid lumps.

3. Once the water is fully incorporated, whisk in the oil. The batter should have a cake batter consistency- not too watery or too thick. Add a little more water if necessary.
4. Allow the batter to rest for at least one hour.
5. Preheat the oven to 450 F / 230 C. Place a cast-iron skillet in the oven and heat for 10 minutes. The skillet should be very hot.
6. Using oven mitts, remove the skillet from the pan and pour 1 teaspoon of olive oil in the skillet. Use a wooden spatula to spread the oil, so the skillet is fully greased.
7. Immediately pour the socca batter into the skillet. Spread the batter into a large circle. It may not cover the full skillet, based on the size of the skillet.
8. Reduce the oven heat to 400 F / 200 C. Bake the socca for 10 minutes until slightly firm.
9. Top the socca crust with the Tomato Tart ingredients and return to the oven and bake for another 20 minutes.

Vegetable Parmentier

Hachis Parmentier, comparable to a French Shepherd's Pie, is a casserole of ground beef, mashed potatoes, and cheese. This vegan version uses ground mushrooms, walnuts, and carrots in place of ground beef for a dish that is both cozy and wholesome. The herbes de Provence accents the flavors of the vegetables, while nutritional yeast gives a slight "cheesy" flavor. You could certainly use store-bought vegan cheese in place of the nutritional yeast for a more classic taste and texture but for simple comfort, it's perfect the way it is. This is the kind of recipe I know I can serve to anyone- picky eaters, non-vegans, strangers, and friends.

6 servings

4 medium / 780 g potatoes, peeled and chopped
1/2 cup / 120 ml oat milk
1 tablespoon of olive oil
1 onion, finely chopped
2 medium carrots, roughly chopped

8 oz / 230 g mushrooms, roughly chopped
½ cup / 30 g walnuts
4 cloves garlic, minced
2 large tomatoes, cubed
2 tablespoons tomato paste
1 tablespoon soy sauce (substitute tamari or coconut aminos for gluten-free)
1 tablespoon nutritional yeast
1 teaspoon herbes de Provence
1 teaspoon truffle oil
Salt and black pepper to taste

1. Cover the potatoes with water in a pot and cook until they soften. Drain the potatoes and mash with the oat milk and salt to taste.
2. Chop the onion, carrots, and mushrooms and then pulse them in a processor, separately, until fine. Set the minced vegetables aside.
3. In the processor, pulse the walnuts and garlic into a crumble and set aside.
4. Heat the olive oil in a frying pan over medium flame and add the onion, giving it a good stir.
5. While the onions are frying, cube the tomatoes.
6. Once the onions have softened, mix in the minced garlic and walnut and fry for 1 minute.
7. Stir in the minced carrots and mushrooms and fry for a few minutes, until the mushrooms give off their juices.
8. Stir in the cubed tomatoes and fry for a couple minutes.
9. Stir in the tomato paste, soy sauce, nutritional yeast, herbes de Provence, and truffle oil and cook for a couple more minutes.
10. Turn off the flame and season the mixture with salt and pepper to taste.
11. Preheat the oven to 400 F / 200 C.
12. Transfer the cooked vegetables to a baking dish and spread to fully cover the bottom of the dish. Spoon the mashed potatoes on top of the vegetables, fully spread over the vegetables, and use a fork to rake the mashed potatoes in a zig-zag pattern- forming peaks.
13. Bake uncovered for 20 minutes, or until the potatoes peak just start to brown, and then serve.

DESSERTS

Cherry Clafoutis

A Clafoutis aux cerises is a custard or flan-like cake baked with cherries. Clafoutis are easy to prepare and can be made with a variety of fruits or even be made savory with vegetables. For this vegan version- cornstarch replaces the eggs, and coconut cream replaces the butter for a decadent, custardy cake with juicy bites of cherries. Be sure to use thick coconut cream at room temperature. Watered-down coconut cream will make the clafoutis less flavorful. The gluten-free version with rice flour will crack a little when baked but tastes just as good. It tastes best after it has cooled to room temperature and sat for a couple of hours. Traditionally, unpitted fresh cherries are used to keep the cherries from bleeding, and the seeds are said to add flavor. You certainly can use pitted cherries and even frozen cherries- if you're worried about children choking on seeds or prefer the ease of chewing. The frozen cherries will bleed into the clafoutis unless they are thawed and allowed to drain first, but I have made it without thawing the cherries, and the flavor was on par, bleeding and all.

6 servings

½ cup / 75 g all-purpose flour (for gluten-free use ½ cup / 60 g rice flour and reduce the cornstarch to 1 tablespoon)
⅓ cup / 70 g sugar
2 tablespoons cornstarch
¼ cup / 30 g almond flour
½ teaspoon salt
1 cup / 240 ml oat milk
3 tablespoons coconut cream, soft at room temperature
1 teaspoon vanilla extract
¼ teaspoon almond extract
3 cups / 420 g cherries, pitted or unpitted

1. Mix the flour, sugar, cornstarch, almond flour, and salt together in a large mixing bowl.
2. Mix the oat milk into the flour mixture, a little at a time, to avoid lumps.

3. Mix the coconut cream, vanilla extract, and almond extract into the batter.
4. Preheat the oven to 350 F / 175 C.
5. Grease a round baking dish with oil and evenly distribute the cherries in the baking dish.
6. Pour the batter in and around the cherries so that the tops of the cherries are visible.
7. Bake the clafoutis for 40 minutes or until firm and the edge, is golden.
8. Allow the clafoutis to cool to room temperature and serve.

Chocolate Fondants

A Fondant au chocolat is comparable to what is called in English- "molten cake" or "lava cake." A simple batter is made with melted dark chocolate, butter, sugar, eggs, and flour, poured into ramekins, lightly baked so that the edges are firm and the center is soft and runny, and then turned out upside down on a plate before serving. My version took more attempts than I can count to master but it was well worth the effort; it is rich, just the right amount of sweet, and when you break into it with a spoon, it oozes onto your plate. Perfection! To make the fondants ahead of time, bake them as usual and then reheat them in a microwave for 10-30 seconds just before serving. Once the batter is made, it must be baked immediately, or it will overly thicken.

4 servings

140g g / 1 heaping cup / about 12 thick squares dark chocolate
½ cup / 120 ml oat milk
2 tablespoons coconut oil
¼ cup / 35 g powdered sugar + more for sprinkling
¼ cup / 30 g all-purpose flour (or equal amount gluten-free all-purpose flour)
½ cup / 120 ml warm water
Cocoa powder for dusting

1. Lightly grease four ramekins with coconut oil. Dump cocoa powder in the ramekins and rotate the ramekins until they are fully coated. Dump the excess cocoa back into its container while lightly tapping the ramekins.

2. Preheat the oven to 400 F / 200 C.
3. In a saucepan over low heat, melt the chocolate squares, oat milk, and coconut oil- stirring frequently.
4. Once the chocolate mixture is fully melted, turn off the heat and stir in the powdered sugar.
5. Sift in the flour and mix well.
6. Pour in the warm water and whisk the mixture until silky smooth.

7. Pour the batter into the dusted ramekins and bake for about 10 minutes or until the edges are firm but the centers are still liquid. Do not allow the centers to firm.
8. Remove the ramekins from the oven and allow them to rest for 10 minutes.
9. Use a knife to scrape around the inside edge of the ramekins, loosening the fondants. Place a plate under each ramekin, then gently flip. Lightly tap the bottom of the ramekin and then carefully lift the ramekin off.
10. Dust the fondants with powdered sugar and serve immediately.

Crème Brûlée

Crème brûlée literally means 'burnt cream' and is made from custard topped with caramelized sugar. A culinary torch is used to scorch the sugar, creating a hard top that satisfyingly cracks when tapped with a spoon. Underneath is the cold and creamy custard, and a perfect spoonful will include mostly custard with a little of the hardened sugar. This vegan recipe uses a mixture of agar powder (vegan gelatin), cornstarch, and thick coconut milk, in place of eggs and heavy cream, to achieve a pleasing custard texture and flavor. It is difficult to torch the sugar top without a culinary torch, but the torches are generally affordable and easy to find. Depending on your oven broiler, you may also be able to broil the sugar on the crème brûlées in the oven (my oven did not work well for this, but others have had success). Another option is to melt the sugar in a saucepan and immediately pour it *onto the custard, although this still doesn't work as well as torching. When allowed to sit for too long, the sugar crust will start to dissolve into liquid, so the crème brûlées should be served shortly after torching.*

4 servings

1 cup / 200 g thick canned coconut milk, coconut cream, or a mixture of the two
1 cup / 240 ml oat milk
¼ cup / 55 g sugar + more for spooning on top
1 tablespoon vanilla extract
2 tablespoons cornstarch
1 teaspoon agar powder
A dash of salt

For the topping:
cane sugar

1. Whisk all the ingredients together in a saucepan, then place the saucepan on the stove and bring to a boil.
2. Boil for 5 minutes, stirring constantly. Pour the pudding into four ramekins or small bowls and refrigerate overnight or for several hours until firm throughout.
3. Dump a generous amount of sugar into each ramekin and then pour most of the sugar back out, leaving a thin but fully coated sugar layer on the pudding.
4. Torch the sugar evenly using a culinary torch. Hold the torch a few inches away from the sugar and move in a sweeping motion so that the sugar browns equally.
5. Place the ramekins in the freezer for a few minutes, and then serve immediately.

Citrons
3€ le kg
fruits non traités

FRANCE

Lemon Sorbet

Sorbet au citron or lemon sorbet is a frozen dessert of sugar syrup and lemon juice. Sorbets were traditionally used as palate cleansers mid-meal in France but have become popular as a dessert or a dessert side. Sorbets can be made with a variety of fruit such as raspberry, strawberry, or melon. Alcohol is often added to keep the sorbet from freezing too firmly. Sorbets are usually already vegan, but I added agar powder (vegan gelatin) to create a smooth sorbet that is easy to scoop and doesn't require a machine or manual churning. Conventionally, more sugar is used, and a higher sugar content creates a smoother sorbet. I find the amount of sugar in this recipe sufficient, but you can use more sugar if you don't like tart desserts. If the sorbet is frozen overnight, it will require a longer thawing time.

4 servings

1 cup / 240 ml water
½ cup / 110 g sugar
½ teaspoon agar powder
1 cup / 240 ml fresh squeezed lemon juice (about 3 large lemons)
½ teaspoon vodka or other clear liquor
2 tablespoons lemon zest

1. Bring the water and sugar to a boil in a saucepan, then stir in the agar powder and boil for 5 minutes.
2. While the sugar syrup cools, grate the lemon zest and squeeze the fresh lemon juice.
3. Once the sugar syrup has cooled to room temperature (don't allow it to harden!), stir in the lemon juice, vodka, and lemon zest.
4. Pour the mixture into a loaf pan or baking dish and freeze for 4 hours.
5. Remove the sorbet from the freezer and let it sit for a few minutes or until just soft enough to scoop.
6. Use an ice cream scoop to scoop and serve the sorbet.
7. *Optional step*: garnish with fresh mint leaves.

Mousse au Chocolat

Mousse au chocolat or chocolate mousse is a classic French bistro dessert and is always a good idea. It is traditionally made with eggs and melted dark chocolate. To replace the whipped egg whites, this vegan version uses aquafaba- the liquid from a can of cooked chickpeas (it doesn't taste like chickpeas!). The aquafaba is whipped until fluffy and then folded into a dark chocolate mixture. The agar powder (vegan gelatin) in the mixture allows the mousse to set, and the result is a rich vegan mousse that makes a delightful spongy sound when you spoon into it. The quality of your chocolate will make a difference in this dessert, so try to find good dark chocolate without too many additives.

4 servings

½ cup / 95ml aquafaba (chickpea can liquid)
¼ teaspoon cream of tartar
10 thick squares / 130 g / about 1 cup dark chocolate
1 cup / 240 ml oat milk
¼ cup / 55 g sugar
1 ½ teaspoons agar powder

1. Pour the aquafaba into a mixing bowl and place in the freezer for a few minutes.
2. Add the cream of tartar to the aquafaba and beat with an electric mixer for about 10 minutes, starting at low speed and gradually increasing the speed. The aquafaba is ready when it forms stiff peaks. Set the whipped aquafaba aside.
3. Melt the dark chocolate in a double boiler or in a bowl placed in a pot of simmering water.
4. Simultaneously, bring the oat milk and sugar to boil in a saucepan. Mix in the agar powder and simmer for a few minutes, whisking continuously.
5. Whisk the oat milk mixture into the melted chocolate.
6. Fold ⅓ of the whipped aquafaba into the chocolate mixture, then repeat twice until the aquafaba is fully incorporated. Do not overmix the mousse.
7. Pour the mousse into four small serving bowls or one large bowl. Refrigerate for at least one hour before serving.

Tarte Tatin

A Tarte tatin is like an upside-down, caramelized apple pie and is named after the French sisters who invented it by accident. The ingredients are simple- a puff pastry crust, sugar, butter, and apples. Caramel is made from the butter and sugar and poured into a baking dish to harden into a glass, the apples are placed on top, and the crust is laid over the apples. I have included a recipe for homemade vegan puff pastry (including homemade vegan butter) that is not difficult to make but does take time. If using a gluten-free all-purpose flour, the dough will crumble a bit while rolling it. That's ok. Just stick any loose pieces of dough back on. **Feel free to use a store-bought vegan-friendly puff pastry for the crust and skip steps 1-5.** *The caramel is made with olive oil and water which is very tasty but feel free to use vegan butter. Either way, the result will be an elegant dessert of golden, plump apples in a crispy, flaky crust. Need I say more?*

6 servings

For the puff pastry: (can substitute vegan- friendly readymade puff pastry)
1 ⅓ cup / 165 g all-purpose flour (or equal amount gluten-free all-purpose flour)
Vegan butter (can substitute ½ cup store-bought vegan butter):
>**⅓ cup / 50 g coconut oil**
>**2 tablespoons of olive oil**
>**1 tablespoon oat milk**
>**1/2 teaspoon white vinegar**
>**1/4 teaspoon salt**
⅓ cup / 80 ml cold water

For the filling:
⅓ cup / 70 g sugar
½ teaspoon water
1 tablespoon of olive oil
6 apples, peeled and quartered
1 teaspoon vanilla extract

1. Make the butter (skip if using store-bought vegan butter): Melt the coconut oil in a saucepan without boiling it and turn off the heat. Whisk in the olive oil, oat milk, vinegar, and salt, and mix well. Pour into a small bowl and refrigerate for two hours or until firm throughout (can be made the night before).

2. Remove the butter from the bowl and chop into cubes. Use your hands to crumble the flour and butter (including any liquid left in the butter bowl) together but allow the butter to stay slightly chunky (this helps give layers to the puff pastry). Mix the water in a little at a time until it forms a dough ball. No need to overmix. Cover and refrigerate the dough for 30 minutes.

3. Shape the dough into a rectangle and roll it out to 3 times its length. Fold the top third down and fold the bottom third up and over the top third, like a letter. Give the dough a quarter turn and roll it out to 3 times its length. Repeat two more times and refrigerate the dough for 30 minutes.

4. Repeat step 3 twice.

5. Roll out the dough into a large circle, about the size of the top diameter of your baking dish. Place the rolled-out dough back in the fridge.

6. Preheat the oven to 375 F / 190 C and place your baking dish in the oven to warm it up. Melt the sugar in a saucepan, with the ½ teaspoon of water, stirring continuously until brown and caramelizing. Immediately

pour the caramel into the warmed baking dish, tilting or spreading, so that the caramel completely coats the bottom of the dish. Set aside for the caramel to harden.

7. Heat the olive oil in a skillet or frying pan, add the apples, and fry for a couple of minutes. Splash the apples with some water, stir in the vanilla, cover, and simmer until the apples start to soften.

8. Arrange the apples on top of the caramel in a circular pattern, moving them around until they all snugly fit.

9. Prick the puff pastry dough all over, then place it on top of the apples. Fold up the edges of the dough. Make a slit in the center of the dough.

10. Bake the Tarte Tatin at 375 F / 190 C for 45 minutes.

11. Allow it to completely cool. Place a serving plate on top of the baking dish and carefully flip the dish over. Rearrange any stray apples and serve.

Thank you for cooking with me!

I'm so happy that you wanted to delve into the exciting world of vegan French cooking with me. I would love to connect with you! Come find me on Instagram **@saralaterpstra** or at **saralaterpstra.com.**

Help me get the word out!

Vegan French Cuisine is still a teeny niche. Almost daily, I get a message from an excited cook, telling me they had no idea vegan French cooking was possible. But it IS possible and fun too, as (I hope) you've seen in this cookbook! By taking a minute to leave me a review, you will help others find and benefit from this book. And feel free to share this book with your friends and family.

How to leave me a review:

Go to any of the following websites and search for 'Vegan French Favorites'. Click on my book in the search results and scroll to the reviews section, where you will find an option to leave a review.

amazon.com

barnesandnoble.com

goodreads.com

You may also be interested in my other cookbook…

Ever struggled with deciding what to serve at a dinner party? Me too. But the French are masters at making simple, pleasing dishes look elegant. In this cookbook, I've carefully curated recipes that will wow your guests and help you host a beautiful dinner, the French way!

The recipes:
-are French or French-inspired
-are entirely plant based and mostly gluten free to accommodate various diets
-can be made ahead of time in an hour or less
-include measurements in both cups and grams or millilitres
-include tips on how to make things faster and easier

Get your copy of The Plant Soirée at **saralaterpstra.com/cookbooks**

Printed in the USA
CPSIA information can be obtained
at www.ICGtesting.com
CBHW041457280124
3785CB00047B/234